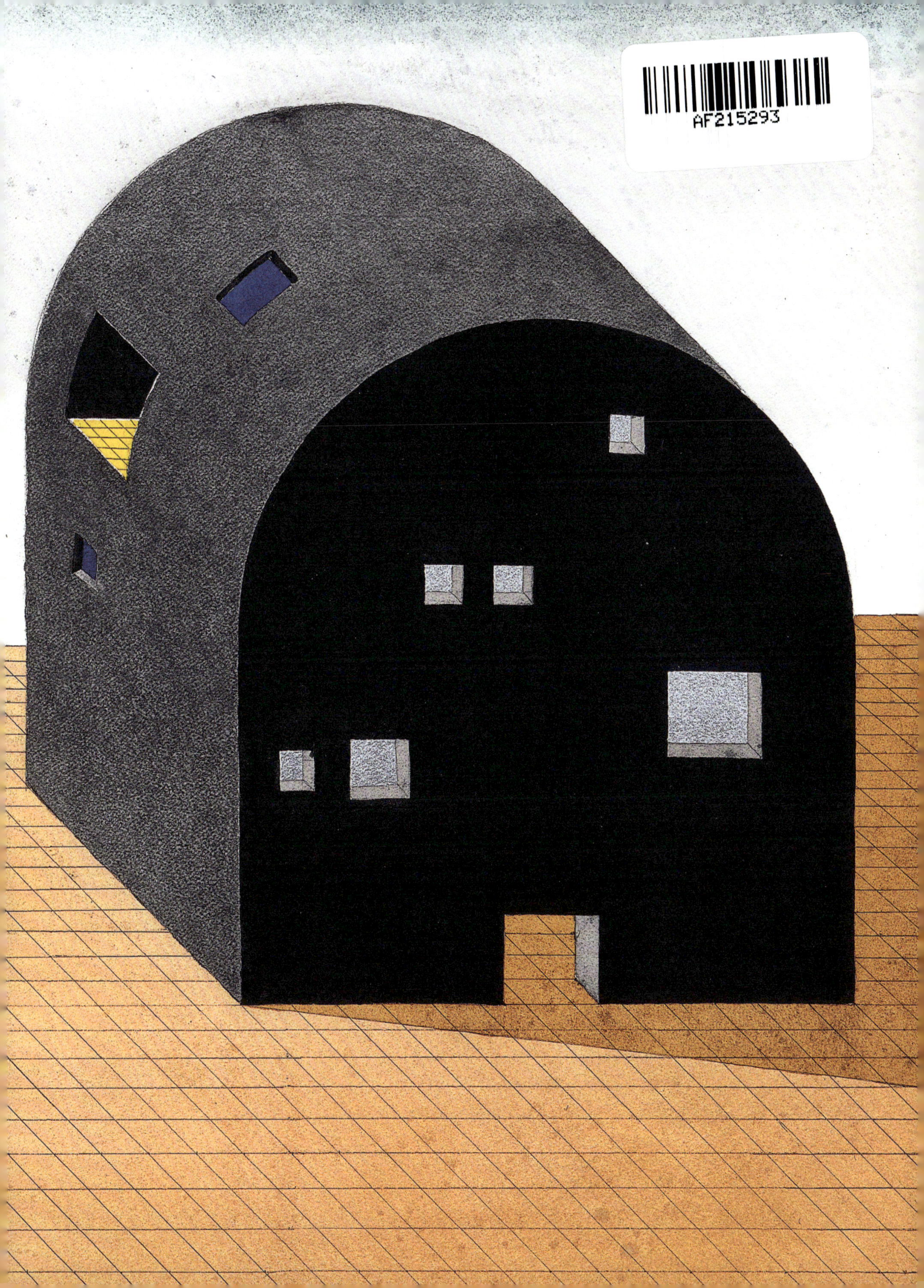

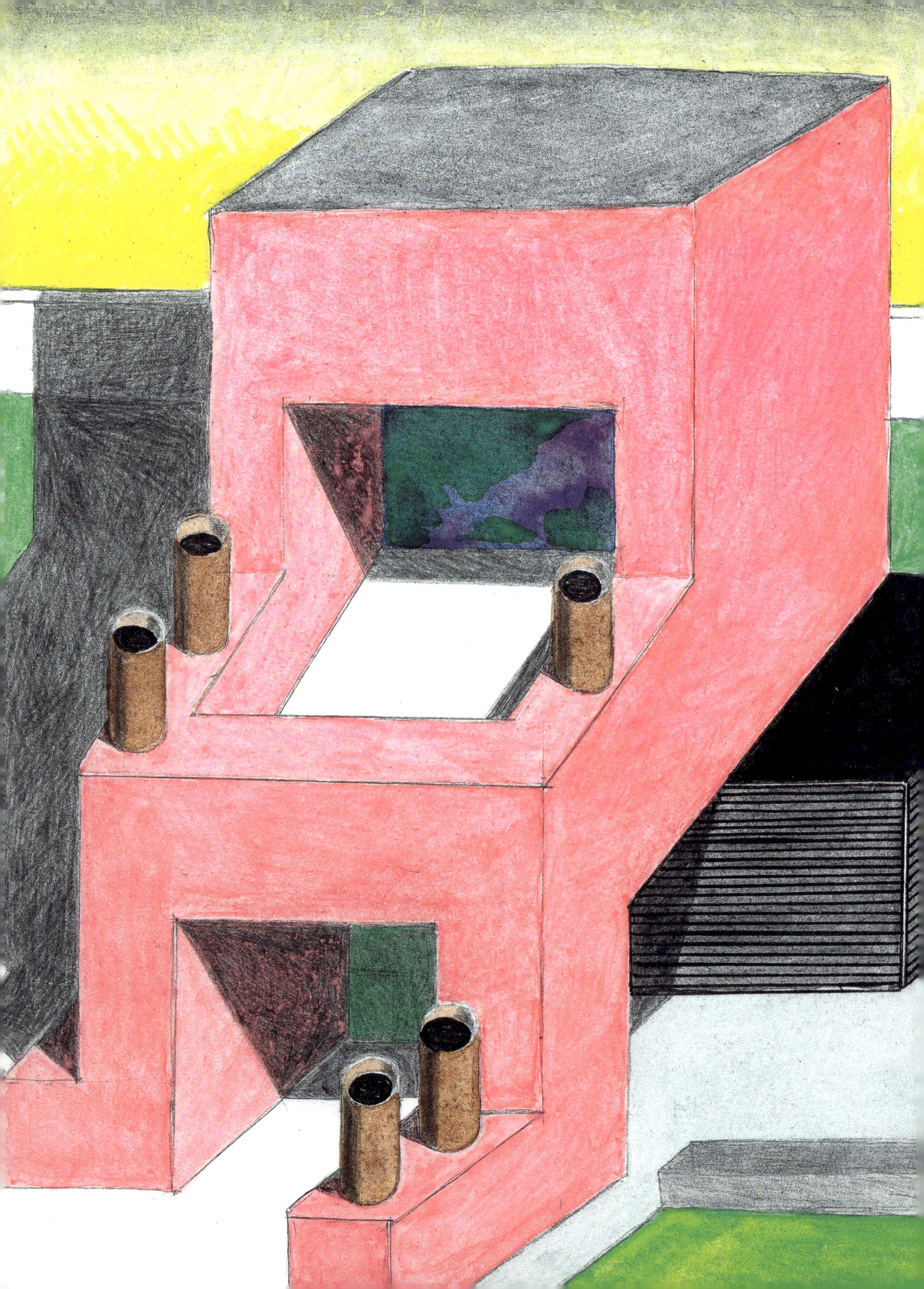

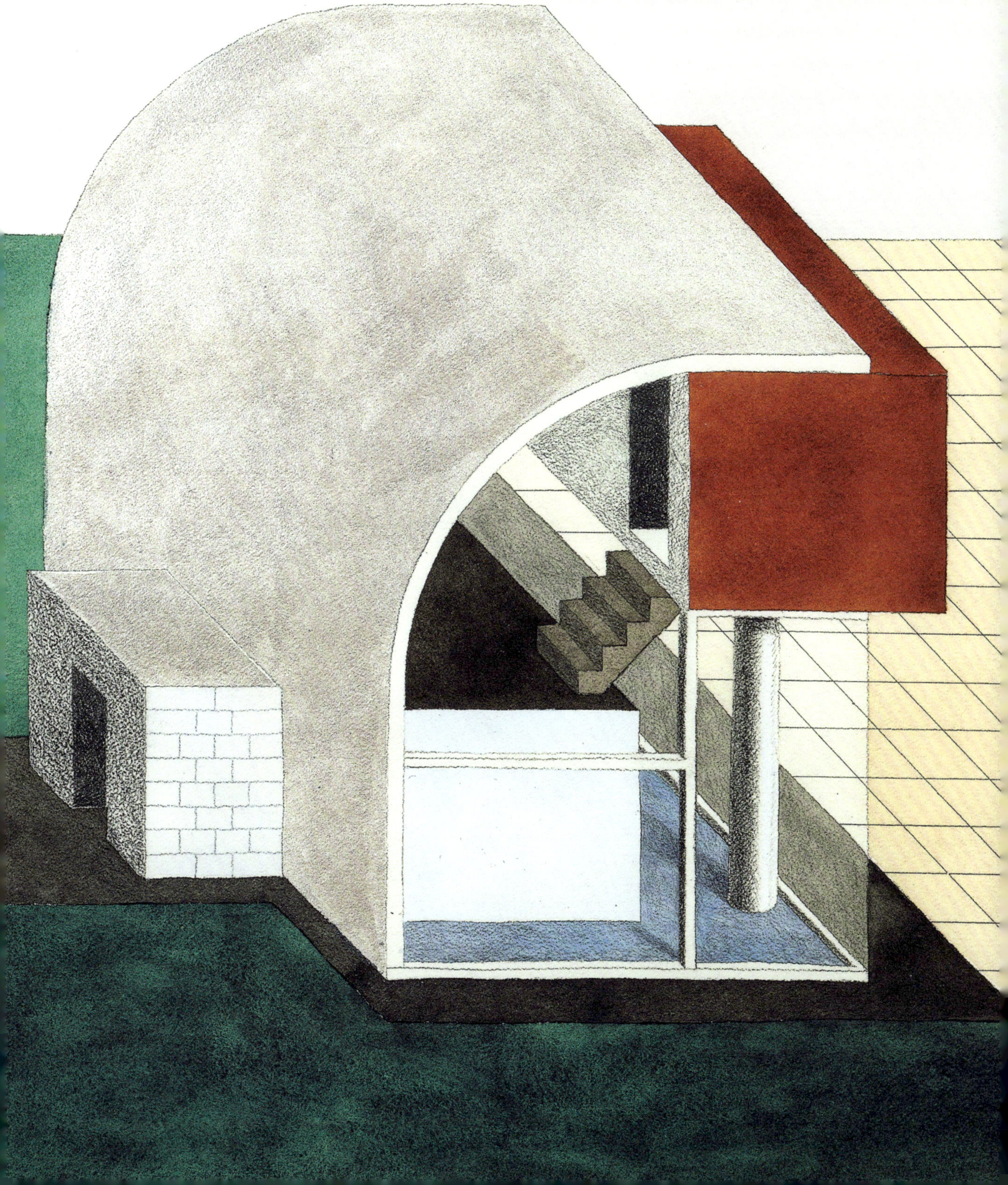

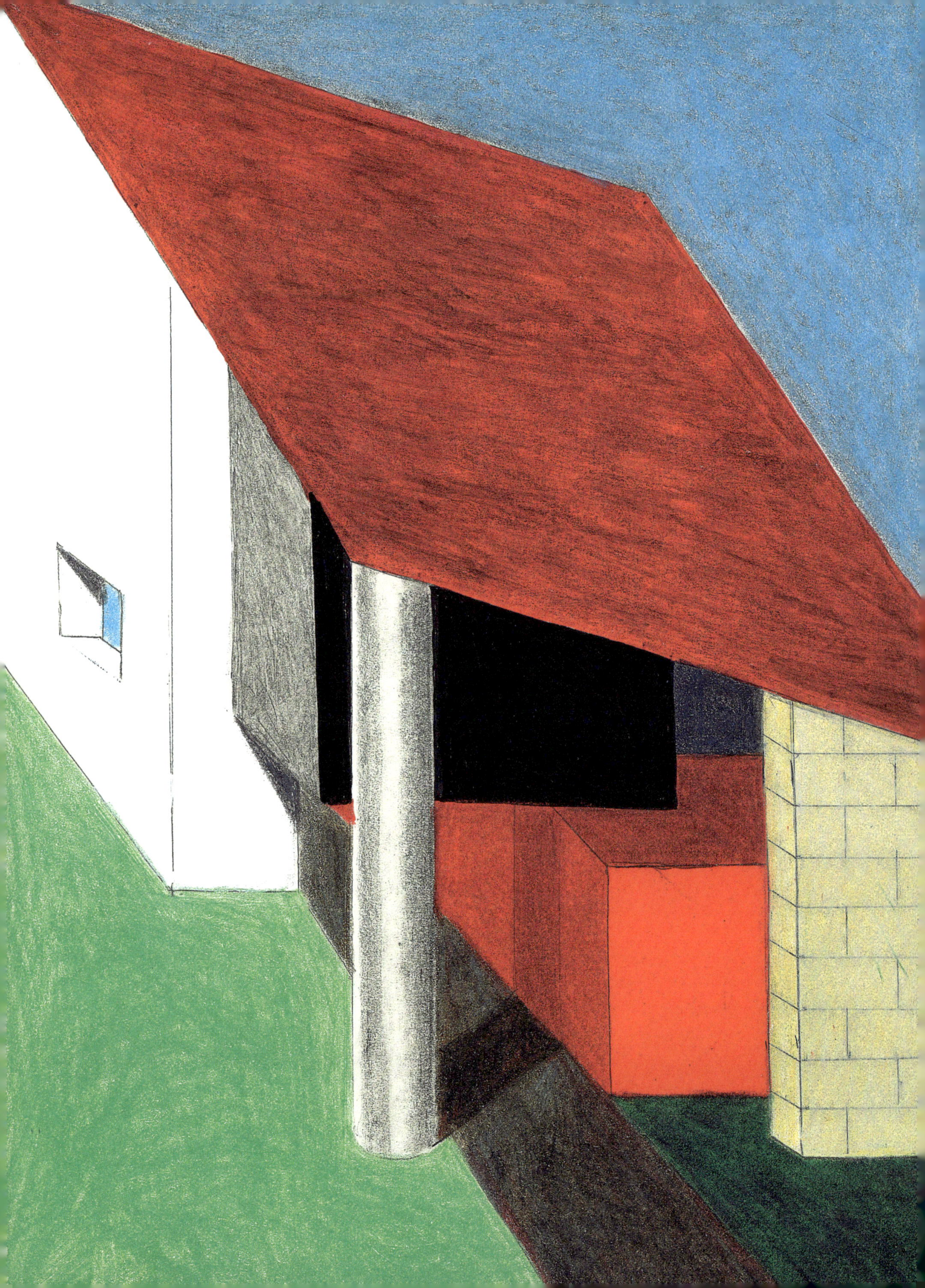

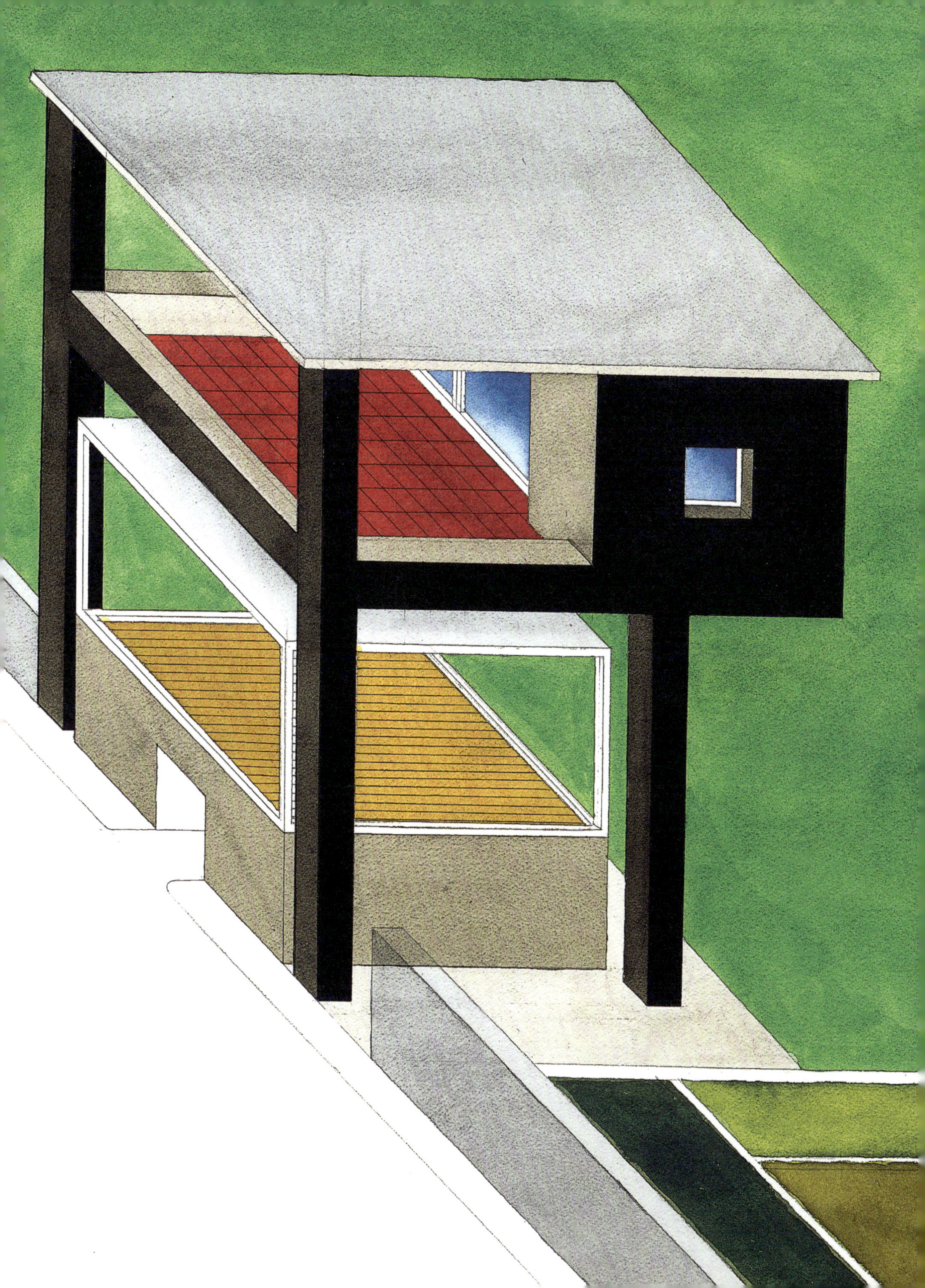

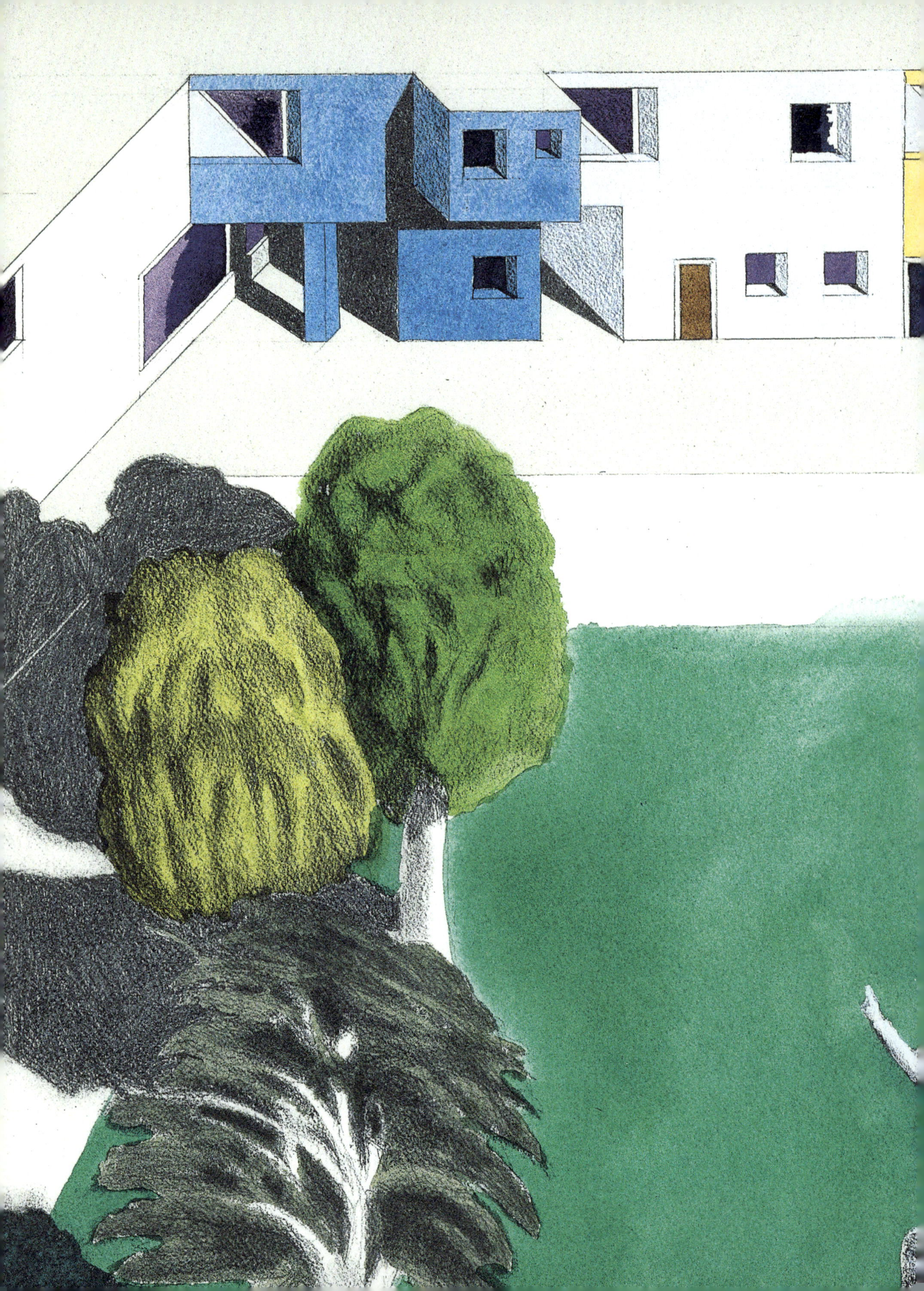

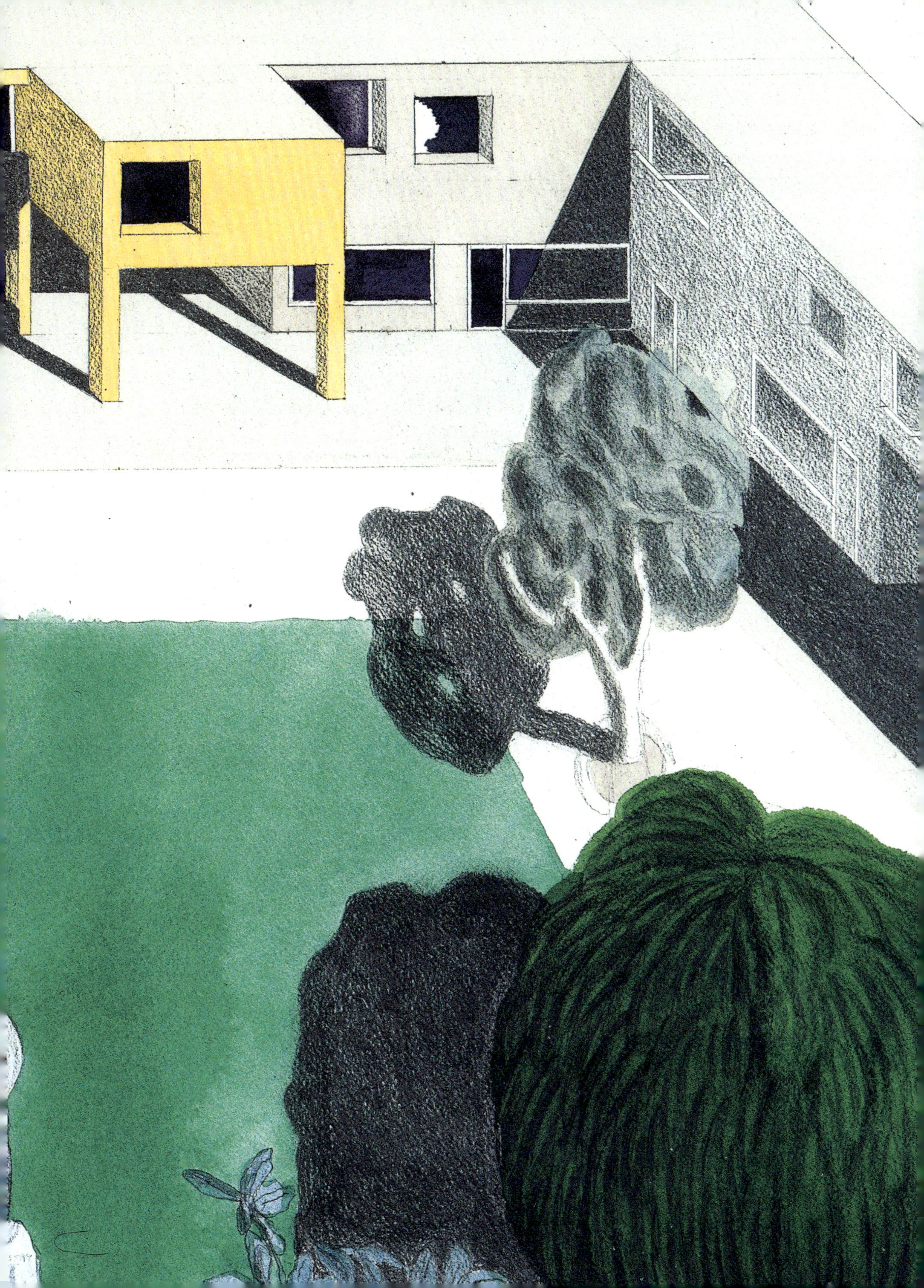

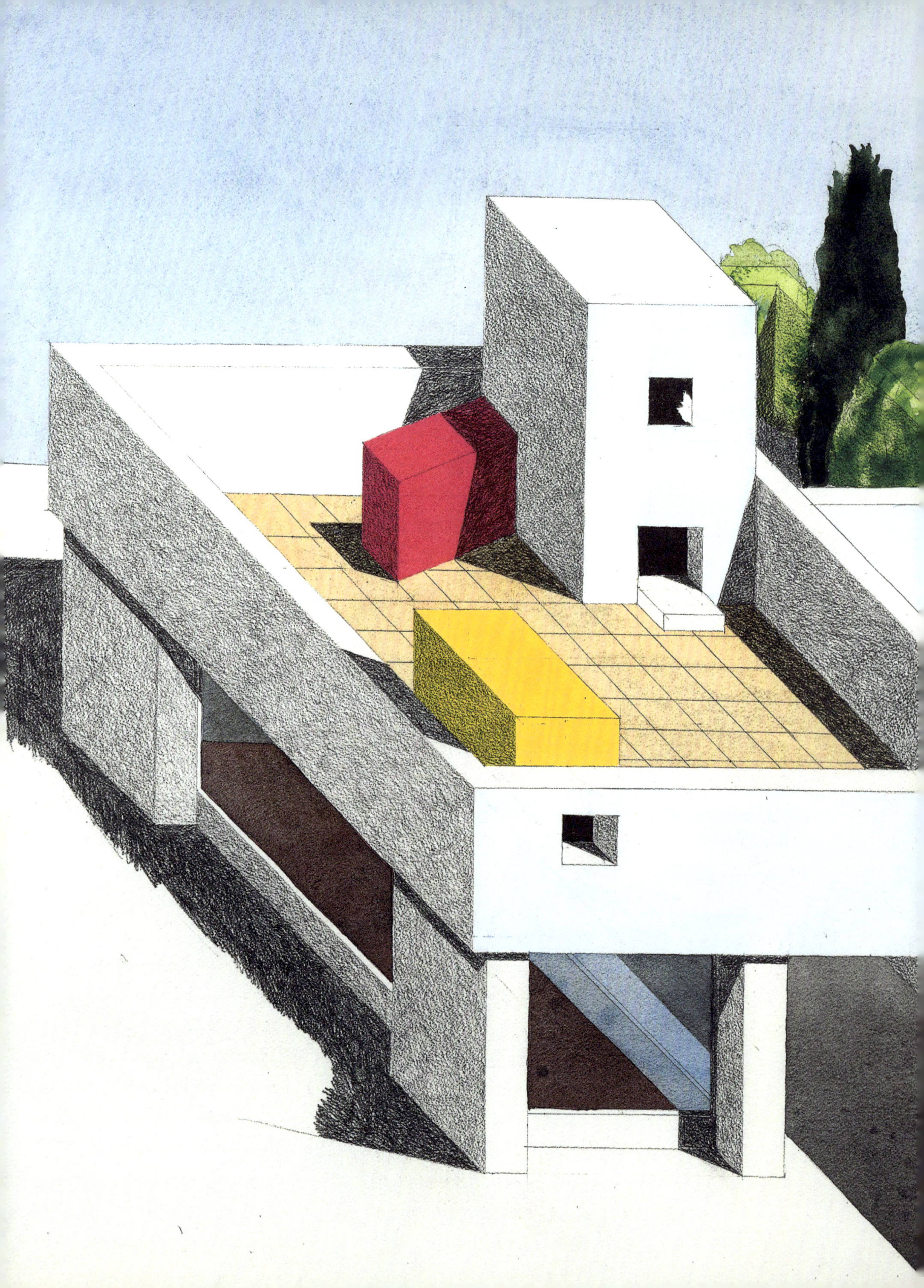

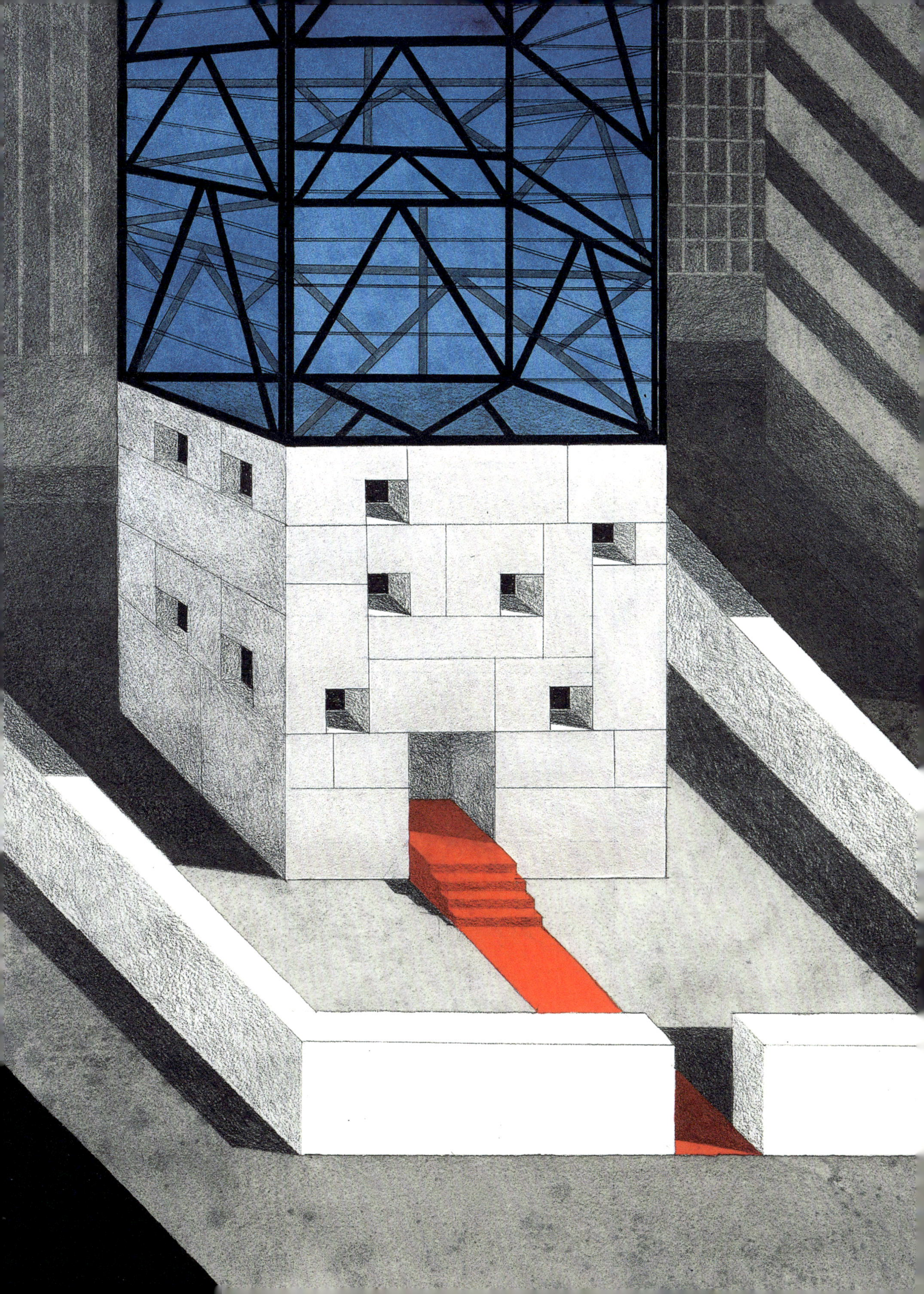

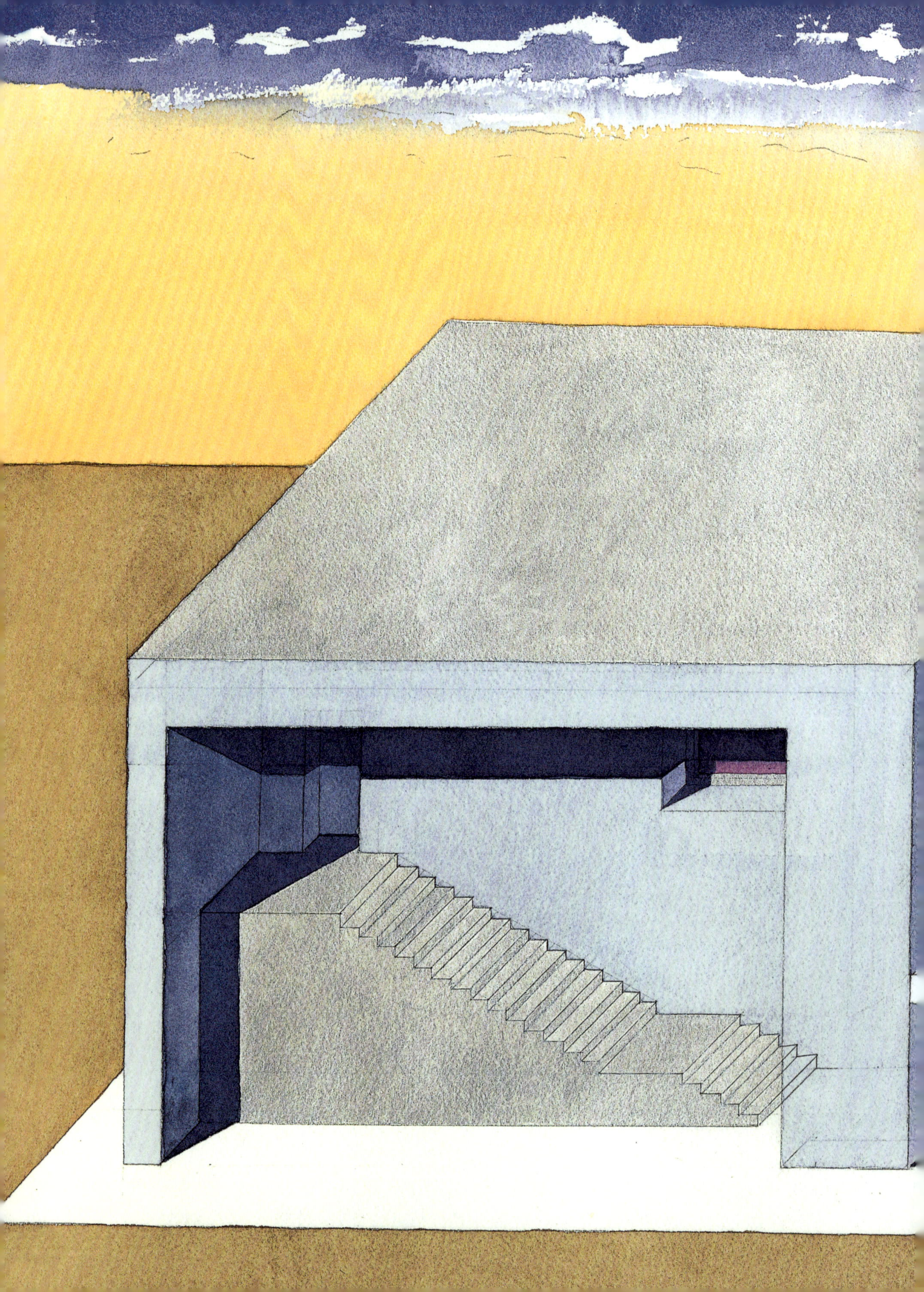

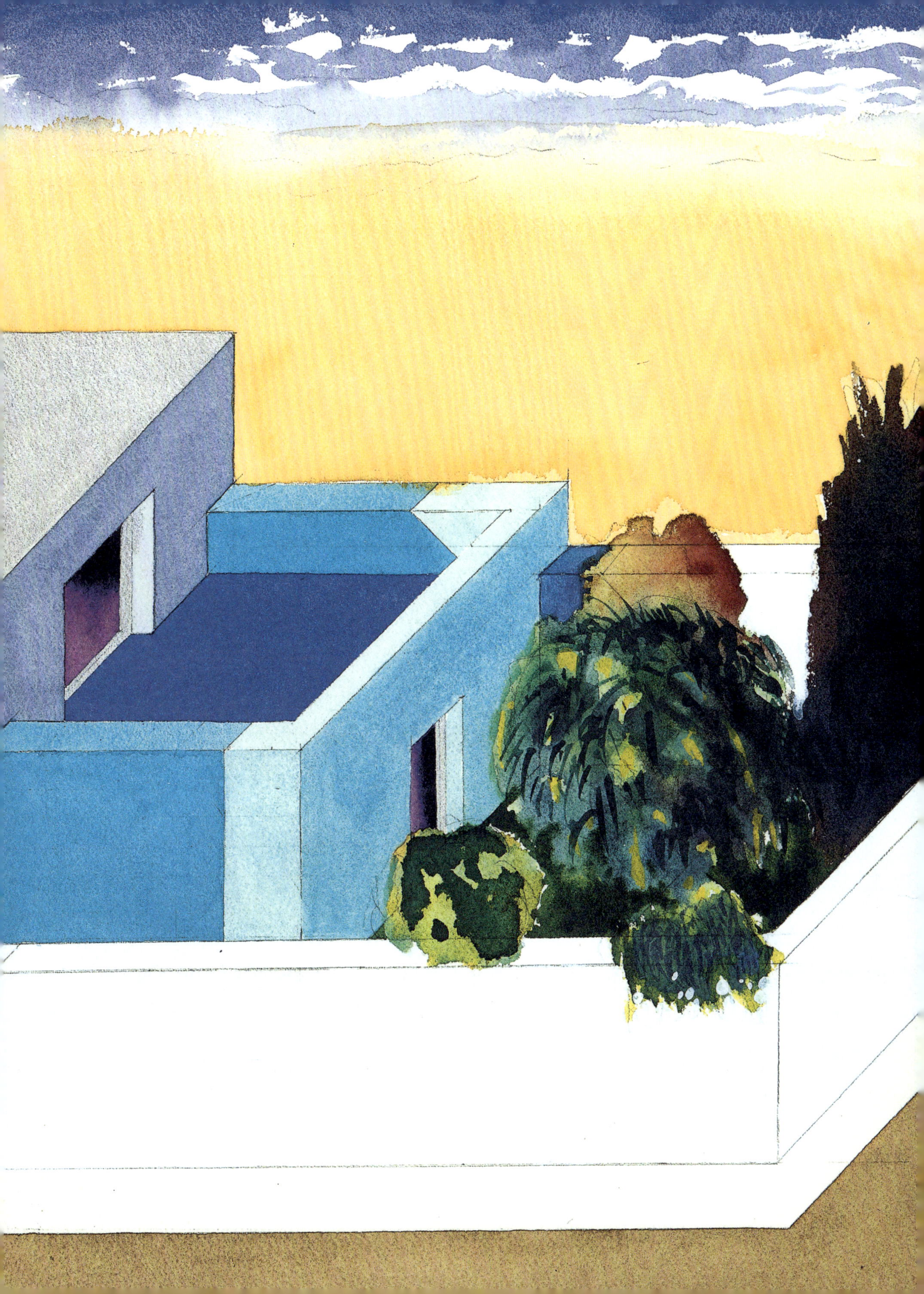

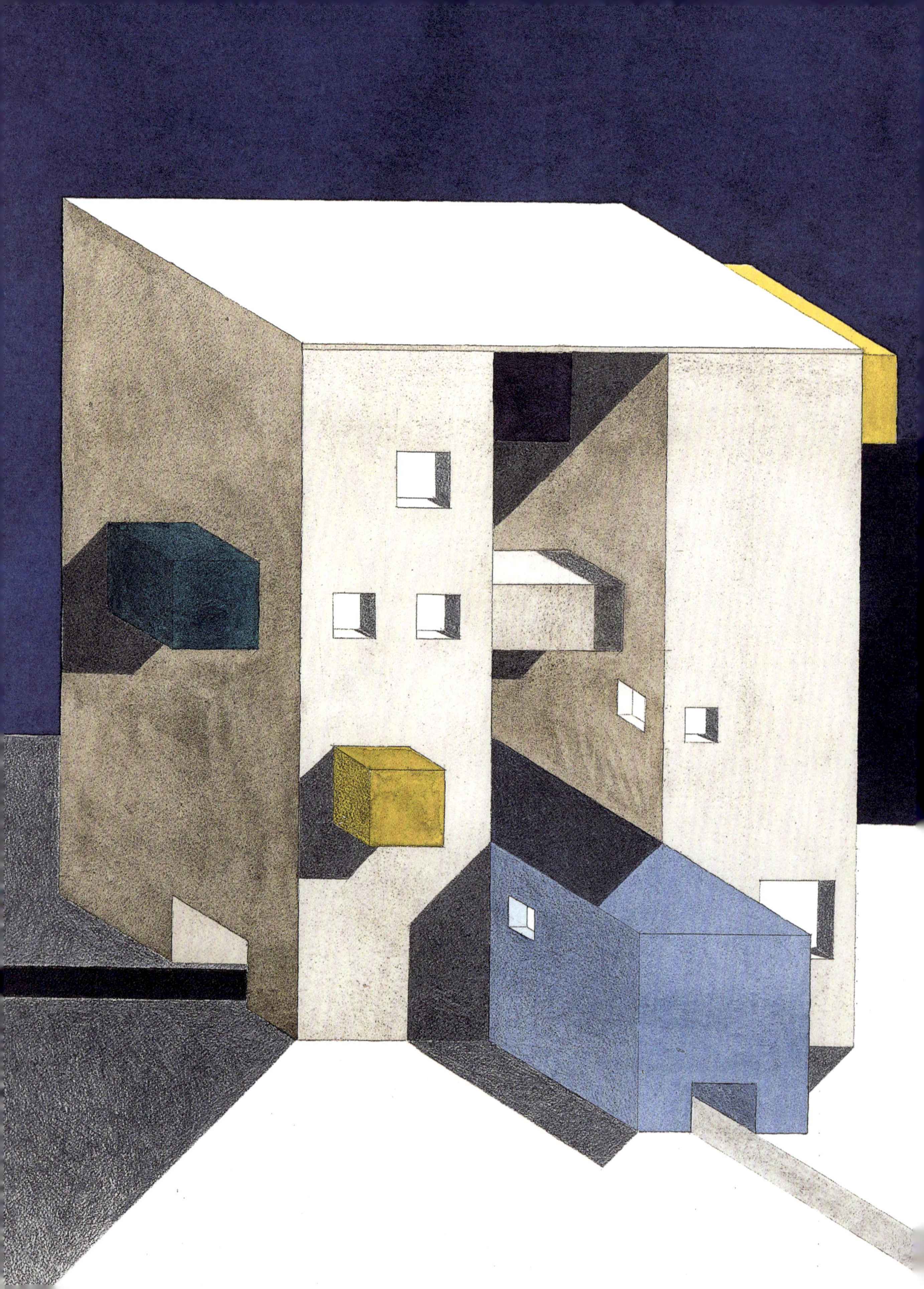

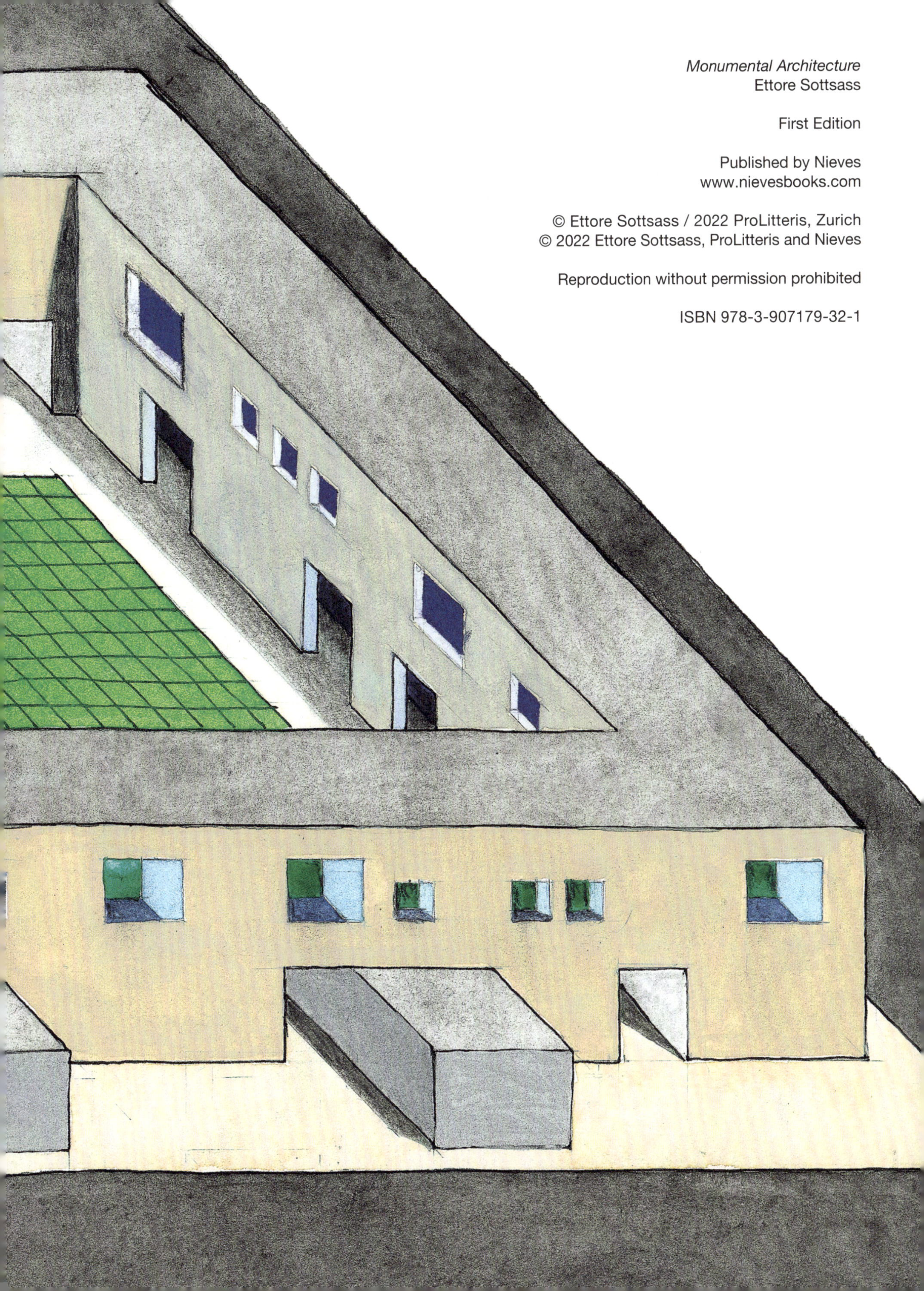

Monumental Architecture
Ettore Sottsass

First Edition

Published by Nieves
www.nievesbooks.com

ISBN 978-3-907179-32-1

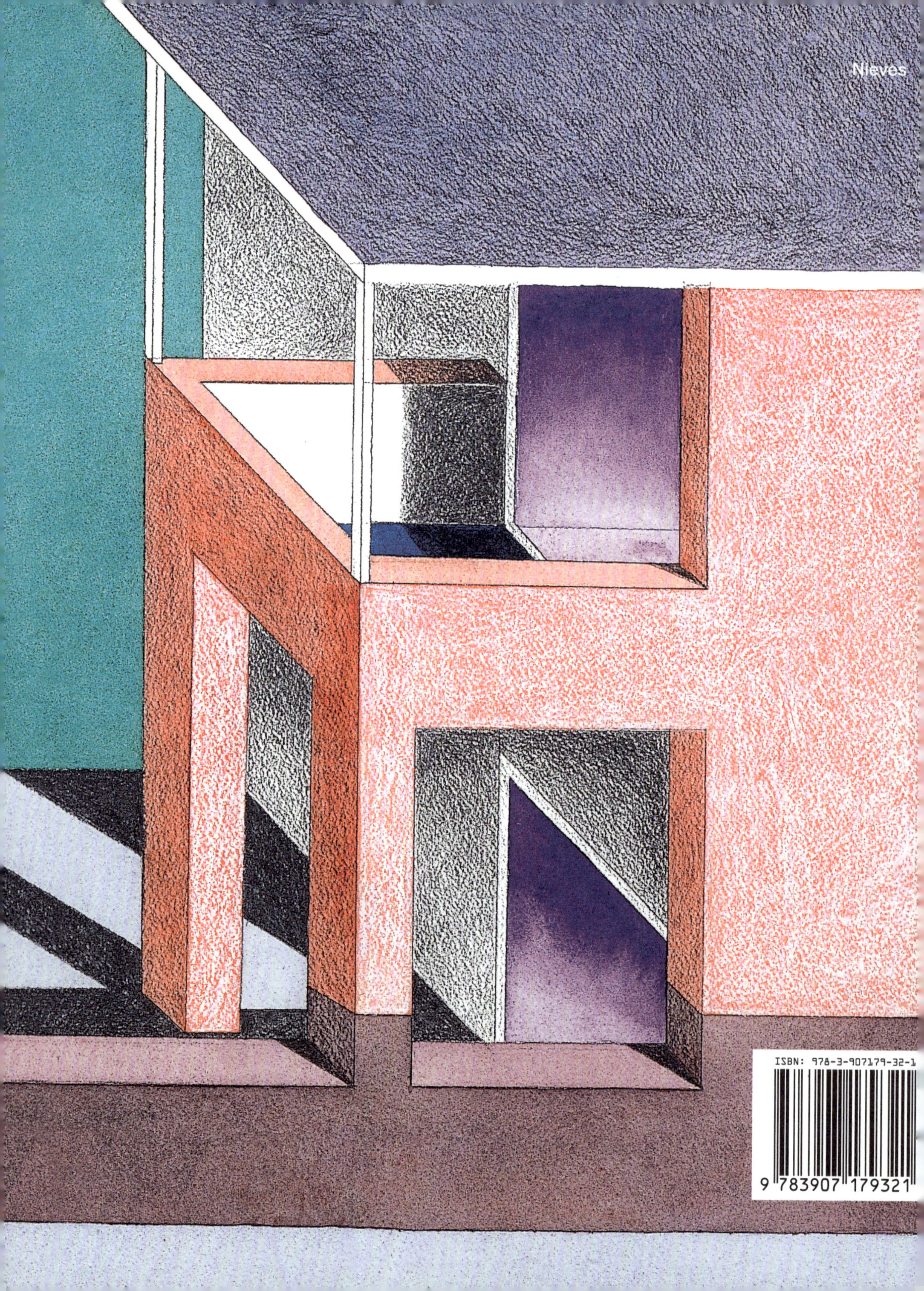

Nieves

ISBN: 978-3-907179-32-1
9 783907 179321

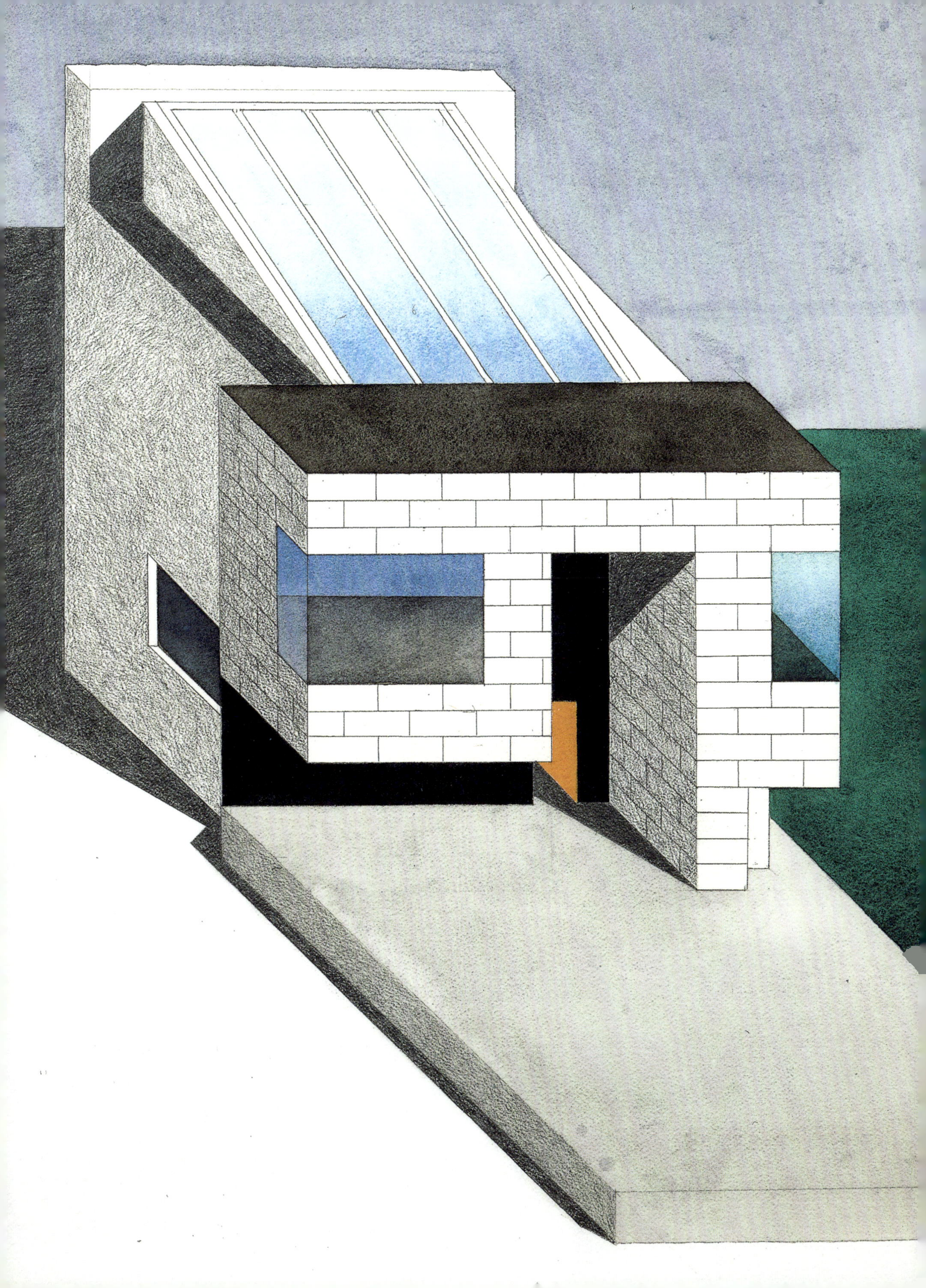

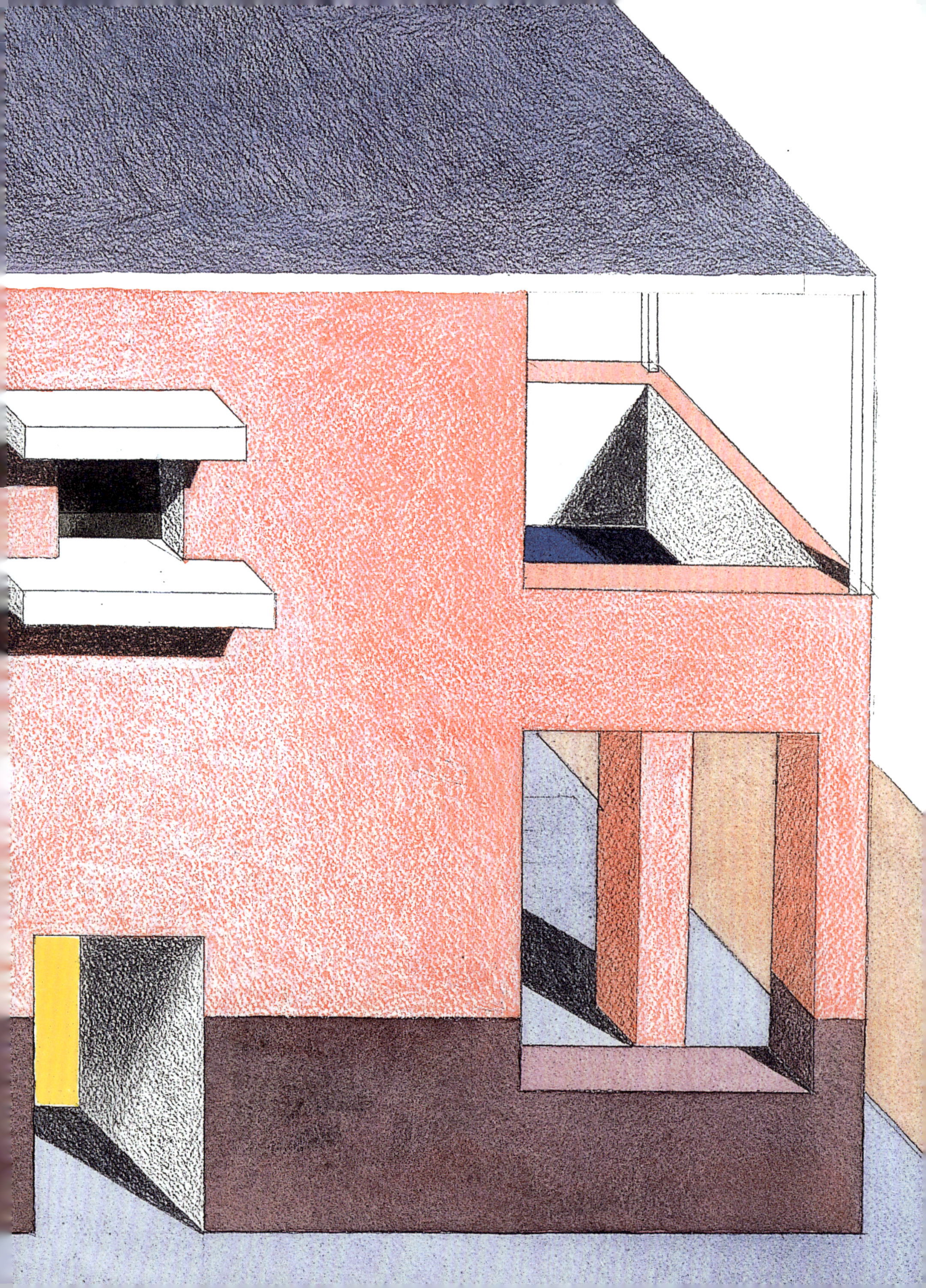